The Yorkshire Coast
& North York Moors

L A N D S C A P E S

John Potter

MYRIAD
LONDON

First published in 2006 by
Myriad Books Limited,
35 Bishopsthorpe Road,
London SE26 4PA

Photographs copyright
© John Potter
Text copyright © John Potter

ISBN 1 904 736 16 5

Designed by Jerry Goldie
Graphic Design
Printed in China

www.myriadbooks.com

Main photograph opposite:
spring showers over the
North Sea at Hornsea

Previous page: winter
sunrise, Robin Hood's Bay

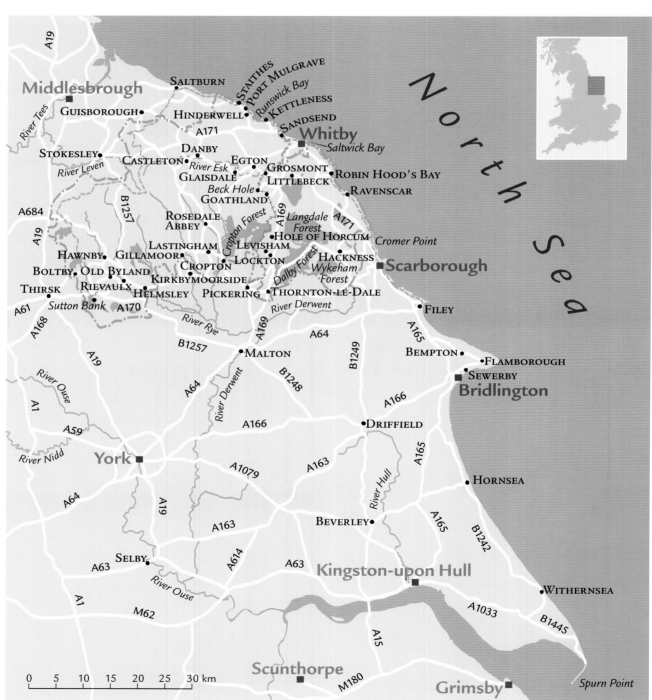

Key
- - - The Cleveland Way
-|-|- The North Yorkshire
Moors Steam Railway
-·- North Yorkshire Moors
National Park boundary
Forests

Contents

THE YORKSHIRE COAST   4

NORTH YORK MOORS EAST   56

NORTH YORK MOORS WEST   98

The Yorkshire Coast

THE YORKSHIRE COAST stretches from the county border at Staithes, just a few kilometres south of the river Tees in Cleveland, to Spurn Point, a long sandy promontory located on the south-eastern tip of the Holderness plain, on the northern banks of the Humber estuary. The North Yorkshire Heritage Coast forms the eastern boundary of the North York Moors National Park. This beautiful and varied landscape is unique with high rugged cliffs, traditional fishing villages, small river inlets and wide sandy bays. The long-distance footpath, the Cleveland Way, hugs the coast from the old smuggling village of Saltburn and finishes south of Scarborough at Filey, passing through some of Britain's most beautiful countryside. The larger fishing towns of Whitby, Scarborough, Bridlington and Filey are steeped in history and charm – so much so that holidaymakers, artists, poets and photographers return again and again, to enjoy this stunningly beautiful region.

Whitby pier *above* and Staithes *right*

4

Staithes

Staithes, known colloquially as "Steers", meaning "landing place", has a very dramatic setting on this rugged stretch of coast north of Whitby. Many of the white painted cottages are haphazardly perched on any available space and the place oozes charm and history. The sheltered harbour is reached from the cobbled main street, at the bottom of the steep hill that winds down from the busy A174 Whitby to Loftus road. Visitors are wise to leave their cars in the car park at the top of the hill and stroll at a leisurely pace down into this unspoilt fishing village.

The Staithes Group

Over the years, relentless storms have taken their toll on the village and some landmarks, such as the original Cod and Lobster pub, and Captain Cook's old shop and home have long since been washed into the sea. The young James Cook received his first taste of the sea and ships at Staithes.

Staithes is a honeypot for poets, writers, artists and photographers. During the late 1890s the so-called Staithes Group of around 30 artists were active in the area, developing the best in British Impressionist painting. Many examples of their work, including paintings by Dame Laura Knight and Joseph Bagshawe, are in major public collections, including Tate Britain in London.

Port Mulgrave

Port Mulgrave is a tiny seaside hamlet between Hinderwell and Staithes. It was formed in the 1850s when ironstone was mined locally. The harbour pier was specially constructed at the time, but is now falling into disrepair as the North Sea takes its relentless toll.

The well-marked path down through Rosedale Cliffs to the harbour is easily found at the end of the minor dead-end road from Hinderwell, but it can be very slippery after rain and visitors should be careful. There are splendid sea views to be had along the Cleveland Way between Staithes and Runswick Bay, particularly at low tide when the rocky outcrops of Rosedale Wyke, Thorndale Shaft, Jet Wyke and Blackenberry Wyke are revealed. The area is popular with fossil-hunters, but it is easy to get cut off, as the sea always reaches the cliffs here.

The Jurassic coast

The stretch of coastline between Staithes and Port Mulgrave is one of the most famous Jurassic sites in northern England. Ammonite specimens and the remains of dinosaurs and other reptiles can be found on the foreshore; the best time to look for them is following winter storms. But beachcombers and fossil-hunters should always take care to check the tide times before setting off on an expedition.

Runswick Bay

Runswick Bay, situated at the foot of cliffs between Staithes and Sandsend, is a very pretty picture postcard fishing village. Full of charm, the village consists of a maze of narrow winding alleys and cobbled paths that weave their way through tiny cottages with lovingly tended gardens. In 1901, when local fishermen got into difficulty in a storm, the women of the village launched the heavy lifeboat themselves to save their menfolk. To the south-east of the village the headland called Kettle Ness is the site of an old Roman lighthouse.

Runswick's cobles

Just above Runswick Bay's long sandy beach the boat park with its many cobles (small wooden fishing boats) is a honeypot for artists and photographers. The village has a tiny Methodist chapel, an Institute – a local meeting place which was opened in 1870 – an old lifeboat house and a former coastguard house with a thatched roof.

Runswick has suffered many times from the ravages of the North Sea and in 1682 a landslide destroyed the entire village with the exception of one cottage. Thankfully no one was hurt as the locals were alerted by two mourners attending a wake, who realised what was about to happen. In 1970 sea wall defences were completed so the settlement is not as vulnerable as it used to be.

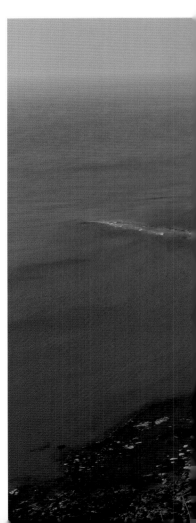

Kettleness

Kettleness can be reached on foot through the hamlet of Goldsborough, which is just west of Lythe on the A174 coast road. There are many headlands on the North Yorkshire coast with the name "ness" or "nose". The cliffs at Kettleness are deeply scarred by both massive landslips and old alum mines. There was a huge landslip in the 19th century, when several clifftop houses were swept down onto the beach. Fortunately it was a Sunday evening and the inhabitants were all in the local Methodist Chapel!

Remains of an ancient Roman signalling station are to be seen in the shape of a large grassy hummock just to the right of the road as it approaches the cliff edge.

Fossil hunting

Sited on Yorkshire's spectacular "Jurassic Coast", Kettleness is
a magnet for fossil-hunters who benefit from a regular supply
of specimens. Because of landslips access to the beach here is
extremely difficult and involves using a rope part-way down the
cliff. A much safer option is to walk from Runswick Bay where
there is a car park. However, the mile and a quarter walk should
only be undertaken after first checking the tide times.

Sandsend *(far right)*

Sandsend is also well known for fossils and the majority are
usually found at the northern end of the beach at the base of
Sandsend Ness. The area is made up of Jurassic shales and
cementstone dating from the Liassic age. Most of the fossils
found are small ammonites. Pieces of jet and fossil wood can
also be found in the cliffs.

Surfer's paradise

Sandsend is a pretty little fishing village located at the foot of Lythe Bank where the sandy beach that begins at Whitby, just two miles to the south, comes to an abrupt end. There are many picturesque stone cottages set against a backdrop of cliffs and beside two meandering streams which flow out onto the long sandy beach.

Sandsend has some of the best surf on this stretch of the coast and has a reputation as a local surfers' paradise. These hardy individuals are often to be seen in all weathers enjoying the huge waves.

If you follow some of the pleasant local walks you will discover the trackbed of the disused coastal railway and the earthworks of Mulgrave Castle hidden away in Mulgrave Woods just inland from the village. Sandsend was once important for the mining of alum and the massive amounts of waste on Sandsend Ness show the results of more than 250 years of quarrying which ended in the middle of the 19th century. You can enjoy a walk along the old railway line through the quarried landscape where nature has now taken over the old mine-workings.

Whitby

Often referred to as Captain Cook's Country, the seaside town of Whitby and the surrounding countryside, from where the young James Cook drew inspiration and learned the seafarer's trade, is steeped in maritime history. Cook was born in Marton, a small village just south of Middlesbrough. His first job was in Staithes, where he assisted the merchant William Sanderson. In 1746 he took up residence in John Walker's house, an elegant 17th-century harbourside house in Grape Lane, where he served his apprenticeship and learned about navigation and seamanship. The house is now a museum which has recently been extended to include a special exhibition entitled *Curiosities from the Endeavour*, a neglected collection not seen for 200 years.

Whitby attractions

Whitby offers a host of things to do throughout the year. There are two "heritage" railways, the Esk Valley Railway Partnership and the North York Moors Railway which are both very popular, particularly with families. The author Bram Stoker (1847-1912) set much of his classic Victorian novel *Dracula* in and around the town and today visitors with a taste for the gothic can retrace the steps of the "undead" by taking the Dracula Trail Tour.

The photographer Frank Meadow Sutcliffe (1853-1941) is Whitby's most famous artist. He immortalised the town and the life of its fishing community in scores of beautiful, sepia-tinted photographs many of which can be seen at the Sutcliffe Gallery, where his work has been on view for over 40 years.

St Hilda's Abbey

Whitby's skyline is dominated by the ruins of St Hilda's Abbey, high up on East Cliff. Just nearby, the parish church of St Mary is one of the finest Anglo-Saxon churches in the north of England. Below the church 199 steps lead down into quaint, winding narrow streets, lined with galleries, cafés, craft shops and tea rooms. Whitby today is a busy, exciting and immensely popular holiday destination for visitors.

Saltwick Bay

If ever a bay could be designed with a landscape photographer or painter in mind then surely this would be it! Saltwick Nab, a low rocky outcrop at the southern end, lies one mile south-east of Whitby. Access to the bay is via a steep winding path that leads down to its soft sandy centre. On either side of this beach are vast rock platforms which are only revealed as the tide recedes. Close to the Nab there is the eerie outcrop known as Black Nab and at the foot of the cliff are old mineworkings and remnants of ancient breakwaters. The area is noted for fossils and the steep cliffs are constantly being eroded by the sea and the weather systems that sweep in from the North Sea.

The place has a real sense of atmosphere, particularly at first light. Many boats have come to grief on the rocks here, the most famous being the HMHS *Rohilla*, a hospital ship of 7,409 tons which belonged to the British India Steam Navigation Company. The ship smashed into a reef near Saltwick Nab on October 29 1914; of the 229 people on board, 62 crew and 28 passengers perished. The rescue took 50 hours, watched by local townspeople on the beach who cheered the rescuers on and waved lanterns.

Robin Hood's Bay

The picturesque, characterful and fascinating fishing village of Robin Hood's Bay is just waiting to be explored. Its steep winding streets and cobbled ginnels (narrow alleyways between houses) are lined with old houses and cottages, many with red pantiled roofs, and everywhere there is the sound of the gulls which nest on the rooftops and chimneystacks. Legend has it that Robin Hood once repelled Danish invaders here; during the 18th century, goods were smuggled ashore by means of secret tunnels below the houses. Robin Hood's Bay is a very popular location for the study of marine life and for fossil-hunting, especially at low tide when the vast expanse of scars are revealed.

The Coast to Coast long-distance trail, originally devised by the distinguished fell-walker and writer Alfred Wainwright, which starts at St Bee's on Cumbria's west coast, finally ends at Robin Hood's Bay. Weary but very contented walkers can often be seen walking down the cobbled jetty and dipping their sore feet into the sea to complete what must be one of the finest long-distance walks in the British Isles. The trail is 190 miles long and walkers typically take around 10-12 days to complete the trek.

Boggle Hole

This oddly named settlement just half a mile south of Robin Hood's Bay is said to have once been a notorious smugglers' haunt. Nowadays you are more likely to find beachcombers of all ages exploring the rockpools for marine life and fossils. First light at Boggle Hole, far left, is a wonderful place from which to see the sunrise over the North Sea. Access to the beach here is relatively easy, with car parking half a mile from the clifftop and a delightful walk through woods then down a steep ravine where the youth hostel is located near the beach. Naturalists will revel in the rich variety of flora and fauna to be found along the inland-running ravines in the area. Just inland are the picturesque villages of Raw and Fylingthorpe.

Ravenscar

Steeped in legend and history, the beautiful stretch of Heritage Coastline from Whitby to Ravenscar is, quite simply, breathtaking. Ravenscar itself is situated high on a rocky headland, which overlooks the wide, sweeping crescent of Robin Hood's Bay. In 1896 the Ravenscar Estate Ltd drew up plans for an ambitious new town to be built. Plots of land were sold and the basic infrastructure laid down by the company. A railway line was constructed and a station built. In the end, though, this unique and windswept location became its own downfall as it proved too challenging for the developers of the day and the town was never built. In fact, during one very severe storm, the entire railway station was blown away!

Ravenscar

Ravenscar is one of the wildest and most exposed places in Yorkshire, being 183m (600ft) above sea level. The winds that blow across the North Sea sweep down from the Arctic Ocean, so it's no surprise that the once planned town was not developed. Today the 18th-century Raven Hall at the top of the cliff is a hotel and, in fact, is situated on the site of a Roman signal point. The headland is now owned by the National Trust. There are fabulous views of the sweeping Robin Hood's Bay from the coastal clifftop path, far right, and, in the distance, Ravenscar headland from Boggle Hole, right.

The long-distance footpath, the Cleveland Way, leads north to Robin Hood's Bay and south to Ravenscar, offering ramblers and holidaymakers an abundance of spectacular views of the sea along this section, and ornithologists are often afforded close sightings of a large variety of seabirds.

Cromer Point

Cromer Point can be reached along Field Lane just east of the village of Burniston, which is 2 miles (3.22km) north of Scalby Mills and Scarborough North Bay. Tremendous views of the distant castle at Scarborough can be enjoyed here, particularly at first light. A dismantled railway track runs parallel to the Cleveland Way along this section of the coastline and provides ramblers with an alternative path to explore.

Surfing
This location is very popular with surfers, as are the coastal resorts of Runswick Bay, Sandsend Bay, Scarborough, Cayton Bay, Filey and Withernsea. Cromer Point is also an excellent spot for birdwatching and many rare species have been sighted there.

Scarborough

Scarborough is one of the north of England's most popular coastal towns, and was in fact Britain's first seaside resort. Anne Bronte died in Scarborough at the young age of 28. She had been seriously ill with consumption and visited the resort with her sister, Charlotte, in the hope that the sea air would cure her condition. She is buried in the graveyard of St Mary's Church.

Founded just over a thousand years ago Scarborough is, historically, a relatively young settlement. Its name is derived from that of Thorgils Skarthi, the Viking raider who settled on this rocky and wild headland.

The lighthouse (right), a harbour beacon, built in 1806 on the end of Vincent's Pier, was all but destroyed by an enemy raid on December 16 1914. The town is divided into two bays, North Bay and South Bay, by a huge headland and castle. These sunrise photographs were taken at South Bay (above) looking south towards Filey and (far right), looking north towards the headland and harbour.

Scarborough views

The ruined Norman castle and its headland dominate Scarborough's skyline. The headland stands 150ft (46m) above the harbour and, as can be seen in the photograph (right), on a clear day a fantastic view can be enjoyed from Oliver's Mount. Below, the Spa Complex with its superb parks, gardens, theatres and conference hall sits majestically beside the principal bathing beach.

Although the harbour is now chiefly used by leisure cruisers and yachts, fish is still landed here. Scarborough became a major fishing port after King Henry II built the castle in the 1170s and this led to the development of the famous Scarborough Fair, a six-week trading festival, which attracted merchants from all over Europe. In the first few decades of the 20th century it was not uncommon to see barrels of fish packed in salt lining Vincent's Pier, before being transported to inland markets for sale.

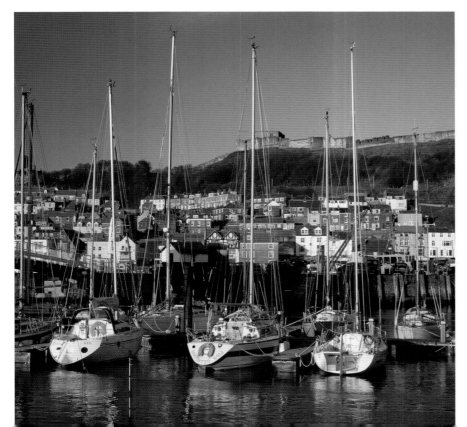

Filey

Filey is an elegant and unspoilt English seaside town. Charlotte Bronte once stayed at Cliff House, now known as the Bronte Café, and other famous visitors include the composer Frederic Delius and the Mountbatten family. The five-mile sandy beach is protected from the north by the magnificent Filey Brigg. Looking back from the Brigg, seen here in the distance (right), one notable feature of the town is the magnificent row of proud Victorian houses called the Crescent. This small and friendly town has many attractions including the cobbles, where small fishing boats rest at jaunty angles outside the popular beachside café. There is a week-long Edwardian festival every year in June, when strawberry teas are served by ladies in period costume. Brass bands, barrel organs and the traditional Punch and Judy show provide fun for all ages.

Bempton

At 400ft (122m), Bempton has some of the highest cliffs on the east coast of Britain, and is famous as a seabird nature reserve, featuring the only gannet colony in mainland Britain. The RSPB bought the cliffs in 1969 and they are situated just north of Flamborough Head, and close to Bridlington. Access for visitors is easy by car or on foot, from the little village of Bempton one mile inland. The village is very peaceful, and has many small and attractive stone cottages and guesthouses, making it an ideal place from which to tour the area. The meadow pipit (photographed right), is a ground-living (terrestrial) bird that looks very much like a small thrush. May and June are particularly good months to see wild flowers on the cliff tops such as the red campion (*Silene dioica*).

Bempton Cliffs

A survey carried out by the RSPB revealed that gannets nesting in Yorkshire had reached an all time high in 2005. The gannet is Britain's largest seabird, and the number nesting at Bempton Cliffs has increased in recent years. In 1969 there were just 21 gannets' nests compared to 3,940 in 2005. Sadly, though, kittiwakes had their worst season in almost 20 years. Puffins (left), are a joy to watch. Their waddling walk and brightly coloured clown-like faces make them a very endearing sight.

Gannets can be seen at Bempton between January and November and are most active between April and August when they are breeding. The Bempton Cliffs nature reserve is open at all times, and the RSPB visitor centre is open daily throughout the year.

Flamborough

The coastline at Flamborough is magnificent: Thornwick Bay (above) is just one of the many sheltered shingle coves fronting the sea, and many have sea caves and dramatic stacks. The cliffs and coves teem with seabirds; the young shag (right) sadly floundered and died on the beach here, probably through exhaustion and hunger, following violent sea storms.

There are two schools of thought as to the origins of the place name. In the Domesday book this part of the coastline is called "Flaneberg", from the Saxon *flaen* meaning dart – a possible reference to the shape of the headland. Alternatively, the name could have developed from "the place of the flame".

Flamborough lighthouse

A lighthouse was first built at Flamborough in 1669 by Sir John Clayton, but it was never kindled. The present lighthouse was built by John Matson of Bridlington in 1806 at a cost of £8,000. It was first lit in the same year on 1st December.

Sewerby

Sewerby village is a tiny hamlet on the coast just two miles north of Bridlington. Sewerby Hall, on the outskirts of the village, is set in 50 acres of landscaped gardens and is a Grade 1 listed building. The house was built between 1714 and 1720 by John Greame. The rooms on the ground floor are in Georgian, Regency and Victorian styles. Today the Orangery and Swinton rooms and their wonderful settings are used for civil marriage ceremonies, piano recitals, concerts, seminars, art workshops and many other activities. On other floors in the house there are exhibitions, galleries and a heritage library.

The park and gardens are teeming with attractions including a zoo, woodland walks, formal gardens (below), and picnic areas. The beach at Sewerby (right), with Bridlington in the distance, is constantly being eroded as can be seen from this large piece of boulder clay.

Bridlington

Bridlington has all the essential ingredients for the perfect holiday resort. There are two glorious long sandy beaches, miles of elegant promenades, a very pretty and bustling harbour, as well as arcades, shops, amusements, restaurants and cafés. Flamborough Head and the lighthouse are clearly visible from the north pier and beach. In recent years the large fleet of trawlers has diminished and now the harbour buzzes with the sound of yachts, private fishing boats, pleasure craft and the very popular *Yorkshire Belle*.

There is a lifeboat housed at Bridlington and it is launched onto a slipway from premises near the Spa Theatre. From there it is towed by tractor onto the beach.

Below and right, still water reflections and warm dawn light combine to create beautiful harbour scenes.

Hornsea

Hornsea is a small seaside resort situated 16 miles (26km) north of Hull and 14 miles (22km) south of Bridlington. The town centre is a conservation area and some of the houses date back to the 15th century. The town is well known for the famous Hornsea Pottery which was first set up in 1949 by Desmond and Colin Rawson. In the late 1960s demand was so great that in 1970 another factory was established in Lancaster. Sadly though in 2000 the factory closed. There is also a folk museum which was established in 1978, and is housed in an 18th-century farmhouse.

Perhaps Hornsea's best known attraction is its Mere. Surprisingly the Mere is the largest freshwater lake in Yorkshire. It covers 467 acres (189ha), compared to Semerwater in the Yorkshire Dales which covers 80 acres (32.5ha). Formed by glacial deposits at the end of the last ice age it is one of many water-filled hollows, a reminder that the area once resembled the Norfolk Broads.

Due to the Mere's close proximity to the North Sea it attracts a wide variety of over-wintering birds, including tufted ducks, goldeneyes and gadwalls. Also of special interest are the reed beds which provide ideal breeding sites for hundreds of pairs of reed warblers. Activities on the Mere for both visitors and locals include rowing, sailing, boat trips and fishing.

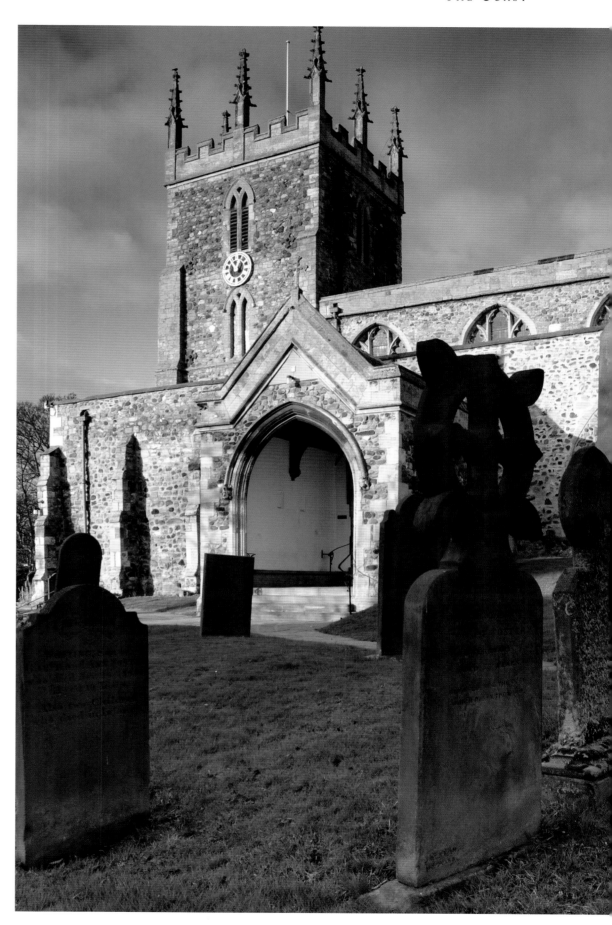

Hornsea Beach

The resort is fringed by attractive pebble and sandy beaches with a newly developed promenade. From the seafront there are spectacular views towards Spurn Head and the entrance to the Humber estuary. The beach lies at one end of the Trans-Pennine Trail which finishes in Southport in Lancashire. The parish church of St Nicholas (right) dates back to the 12th century and is located in a busy street in the town centre. Famous visitors to this charming resort include Lawrence of Arabia and local novelist Winifred Holt.

Withernsea

Withernsea lighthouse is most unusual in that it stands in the middle of the town. Even as far back as the 1800s people were concerned about coastal erosion. Climb the 144 steps to the lamp room at the top and breathtaking views are to be had of the town and surrounding countryside. The base of the lighthouse has both RNLI and HM Coastguard exhibits. There is also a local history room with Victorian and Edwardian photographs including the railway and pier. The Fifties' film star Kay Kendall was born in the town and there is a memorial to her. Her grandfather, Robert Drewery, was the coxswain of the last rowing lifeboat and helped to lay the foundations of the lighthouse. It was built between 1892 and 1894 and stands 127ft (38m) high.

Spurn Point

Spurn Point, situated on the north bank of the entrance to the river Humber, is a beautiful and unique place. The three-mile long finger of land that snakes out into the Humber estuary is constantly being reshaped by coastal erosion. Sea currents in this area are extremely strong and occasionally seals and porpoises can be seen here.

Spurn Point is a very important location for shipping in the area as it is the home of the Humber lighthouse, Humber pilots and the VTS (Vessel Traffic Services). Spurn Bird Observatory was opened to visitors in 1946 and since then has provided birdwatchers with an ideal location from which to observe and study spring and autumn migration patterns, especially when there is a bracing easterly blowing.

Spurn Point Lighthouse

This 128ft (39m) high lighthouse with its traditional light became redundant in 1985. When in use the light, at 120ft (36m) above sea level, was visible for 17 miles (27km). First records of guiding lights at Spurn show that beacons were erected here by Richard Readbarrow in 1428.

The Bridge and the Deep

The Humber Bridge (left) was designed and built to cross the last major estuary without a bridge in Britain. The north tower of this beautiful suspension bridge is sited on the high-water line and the south tower founded in shallow water 1,650ft (500m) from the shore. It is an amazing example of engineering and was developed from a design originally used for the Severn Bridge. The Humber Bridge was built to serve the communities of both north Lincolnshire and Humberside. Industry and local businesses in towns such as Immingham and Grimsby have benefited from a link to the major port of Hull and motorway connections to Manchester, Leeds and Liverpool.

The gleaming glass and aluminium marine life centre called The Deep (above and right) opened in 2002. Designed by architect Sir Terry Farrell it stands at the confluence of the rivers Hull and Humber and is part of the vision of regeneration for the city of Hull. It was conceived to entertain and educate its visitors about the world's oceans and is an extremely popular visitor attraction, as well as being a unique and spectacular landmark.

Hull's History

Although Hull is not mentioned in the Domesday Book people were trading from the point where the river Hull joins the river Humber long before 1066. By the middle ages a port had developed on the west bank of the river and defensive walls were constructed to the west and north. Because of its growing status Edward I granted a charter in 1299 and from then on the town was known as "Kingston on Hull".

The Hull marina complex (right), was constructed in 1983 and occupies the site of the former Humber and Railway docks. Located in the heart of the city, today the marina is a haven for sailing craft and yachts of all types and provides over 250 permanent berths. The large black boat (right), is the old Spurn Light Boat.

On Princess Dock Street is Hull Trinity House School, which opened in February 1787. It had 36 pupils and the headmaster was the Revd T O Rogers (1787–1789), curate of nearby Sculcoats Church. There was no set curriculum initially but there is no doubt that arithmetic and navigation were among the main subjects. The motto over the door reads *spes super sydera*, which means "hope beyond the stars".

54

The Mission pub (left),
was once a seaman's
chapel. Opened in 1908
it provided a religious
and social centre for the
many seafarers passing
through the port of
Hull. Refurbished in
1995 complete with
pulpit and stained-glass
windows from the
original chapel, it is
now a very popular
haunt for students in
the old town.

The glass-covered
Princes Quay Shopping
Centre (right) is built
on stilts over the site of
the old Prince's Dock.

North York Moors East

FROM THE PICTURESQUE and peaceful Esk Valley in the north of this region, to the vast forests of Cropton, Wykeham, Dalby and Langdale in the south, the landscape of the eastern part of the North York Moors is unique, often diverse, and extremely beautiful. The region is mostly managed for grouse and the heather is regenerated regularly by rotational burning during the winter months. There is extensive sheep grazing across the region and most flocks are reared naturally on farms along the edge of the moor in steep-sided, flat-bottomed green and fertile dales. The moorland vegetation supports large breeding populations of wading birds such as curlew, golden plover and lapwing. Also to be found on the moors are peregrine as well as merlin. A rarely seen bird, the merlin was once the hunting bird of noblewomen in the middle ages.

Above: the Hole of Horcum and, *right*, Hutton Le Hole

Scaling Dam Reservoir

The peaceful and beautiful Scaling Dam Reservoir lies just off the A171 between Guisborough and Whitby. It is the home of Scaling Dam Sailing Club which first opened in 1971. Since then it has been a thriving sailing club, offering the ideal place for families to learn to sail in safety. A wide variety of sports take place on the reservoir including general cruising, competitive races, windsurfing and fishing. Scaling is set amidst beautiful wild heather moorland, and it is a very important location for wildfowl. Part of the reservoir is protected as a nature reserve. There are good parking facilities at both ends of the reservoir, and in the summer a tea van is usually parked throughout the day at the eastern car park. The photograph (below) was taken late on a May evening just before sunset, from the eastern side of the reservoir.

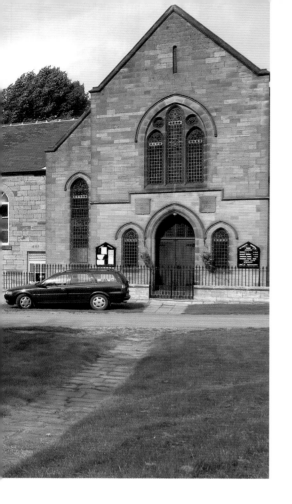

Danby (above & right)

Danby nestles in a hollow at the western head of the beautiful
Esk Valley where Stone Age settlements have been discovered.
Due to its high location the village was once part of a national
network of points where fires were lit when communities were
threatened. In the Second World War Danby was the site of a radar
station that tracked incoming enemy planes. The very first enemy
aircraft to be shot down by wartime hero Group Captain Peter
Townsend was tracked from Danby.

A ruined castle, working watermill, and manorial courts testify
to the significance of this settlement over a long period of time.
The village today has a wide variety of amenities including a village
store, post office, bakery and café, several farmhouses that cater for
visitors, an inn, a tourist information centre and a railway station on
the Middlesbrough to Whitby mainline. The Danby Show is an
extremely popular event for the local farming community and
thousands of visitors flock to the village each year to soak up the
atmosphere, admire the livestock and enjoy the events.

Egton

The two pretty villages of Egton and Egton Bridge on the northern fringe of the North York Moors are situated south of the A171 between Glaisdale and Grosmont, only five miles from the sea. Egton was once a large and important town in the area. The Egton Horse and Agricultural Show, a major event each August, is the largest agricultural show in the area and draws visitors from all around the country. Visitors are well advised to bring wellies as the show is often famously wet! Come rain or shine, there is always fun to be had, especially at the fairground across the road from the main showground.

Egton Bridge, a short walk south of Egton, is set in beautiful mature woodlands at the heart of the Esk valley. The stone bridge which crosses the river Esk was washed away by floods in the 1930s and rebuilt in 1992 in the same style as the original. The village also has a stop on the Middlesbrough to Whitby railway line. St Hedda's RC church is a particularly interesting and ornate building, with an almost cathedral-like interior. It is well worth visiting for the Stations of the Cross and its shrine to the locally-born Catholic martyr the Venerable Nicholas Postgate, who was hung, drawn and quartered in York in 1679.

Opposite: A traditional wood-turning demonstration at the Egton Show

Glaisdale

Nestling in the Esk Valley, the village of Glaisdale is a past winner of "Village of the Year" for the North of England. The valley around Glaisdale is truly a majestic sight when viewed in winter from high up on the fellside (far left). The photograph (above) was taken from the roadside near Low Gill Beck Farm, looking towards Glaisdale Moor. The area once had an abundance of iron ore and in the mid 19th century three blast furnaces were built there. Over time these became uneconomical and could not compete with steelworks with much easier access to transport and raw materials. A railway was planned to capitalise on the valley's potential as a trading centre. Affectionately known locally as "Paddy Waddle's Railway" it was never finished as funds ran out.

There are two bridges over the beck in the valley bottom. One is constructed chiefly from metal and the other, called the Beggar's Bridge, is an attractive stone-built, high-arched packhorse bridge built by Thomas Ferries in 1619. He pledged to build the bridge when, during a flood, he was not able to visit his beloved Agnes, daughter of a local landowner.

Fryup Dale

This quaintly-named corner of North Yorkshire consists of two secluded valleys, Great and Little Fryup, made up of a scattering of farms and cottages. Winding off the Esk valley the area is totally unspoilt and surrounded by magnificent purple heather-clad moors with trails and walks across the moorland. Fryup Dale is an ideal place from which to explore *Heartbeat* country, either on foot or by bike. The picturesque fishing village of Runswick Bay is just 10 miles away and the Esk Valley railway line links with the North York Moors Steam Railway at Grosmont. In early May local farmers need to keep a watchful eye on their young lambs around the clock, especially when bitterly cold weather systems blow down from the north-east.

Grosmont

Situated in the heart of the Esk Valley, Grosmont was originally Grandimont, which takes its name from a small priory founded around 1200. The priory once stood near the north bank of the river Esk but sadly there are no remains to be seen today. The Low Bride Stones, situated on the edge of Goathland Moor at Sheep House Rigg, is a local attraction for visitors – the views into Esk Dale are glorious from this location.

The hillside village of Grosmont is the northern terminus for the North York Moors Railway. The village owes its existence to the railway; during the 1830s, when the railway was under construction, a rich deposit of iron was discovered during the building of a tunnel. A bustling industrial community soon developed around the railhead with brickworks, limekilns and blast furnaces. By 1870 the population of Grosmont had mushroomed to over 1,500 people. By the end of the 19th century the ironworks had disappeared but the village still relied entirely on the railway for food, fuel and everyday necessities. It was not until 1951 that cash was raised by the villagers to build a road that linked them to the outside world.

Steam nostalgia

Grosmont Station has been beautifully
restored to the British Railways style of
the 1960s. Robert Hilliam (top left) a
retired local government officer from East
Ayton near Scarborough,
has worked as a volunteer on the railway
for over five years. The success of the
railway, which now carries upwards of
20,000 passengers a year, very much
depends on the magnificent work of
volunteers like Robert.

Littlebeck

The tiny hamlet of Littlebeck (below) which derives its name from Little Beck, a tributary of the River Esk, lies hidden away in a very deep secluded valley on the edge of Littlebeck Wood. The roads surrounding the village have names such as Goathland Banks, Lousy Hill and Blue Bank, all of which convey the steeply-sided nature of the approach. Reaching the village is quite tricky as the roads are very narrow and caution is recommended. At the bottom of the valley there is a tiny chapel and a ford across Little Beck. A house in the village was once a school with only 13 pupils. Their teacher, who travelled by car from Whitby each day, suffered from arthritis and when the stream was in flood, and she could not cross the ford, school would be held in the village pub!

A very pleasant woodland walk through Little Beck Wood towards the head of the valley and May Beck Wood leads to the long abandoned Midge Hall and Falling Foss Waterfall. The waterfall is located in

a 30ft-deep gorge and access to the base of the falls is extremely tricky and should not be attempted. Midge Hall (above), a derelict farmhouse, is quite an eerie building and has not been inhabited for several decades. It is located just above the waterfall.

Goathland

Goathland is a pretty village situated due north of Pickering. It is immensely popular with visitors who are drawn to the village because of its *Heartbeat* associations – in the series the village is the fictional Aidensfield and many of the landmarks shown in the programmes can be easily identified in a short walk around the centre of the village, including the railway station, which also featured in *Harry Potter and the Philosopher's Stone.*

Beck Hole

Beck Hole is one of Yorkshire's most well-known and best-loved villages. Hidden away in a narrow wooded valley between Goathland and Grosmont, this tiny hamlet is renowned for its inn by the stone bridge and the many delightful walks that can be taken when exploring the area. In the early days of steam, on some of the steepest inclines, railway carriages were drawn by either one or two horses. Such was the severity of the slope that one particular stretch of line between Beck Hole and Goathland used a stationary engine. The Beck Hole rope winch remained in use until a fatal accident in 1864 when the rope snapped! In 1965, when many rural railway lines were closed as part of the Beeching Plan, the Pickering to Whitby line was axed after 130 years of service. Following a public outcry and a protest campaign by the Yorkshire Moors Preservation Society, British Rail sold back the first stretch of track to the Society in 1968.

Opposite: Mallyan Spout waterfall

Goathland

The village of Goathland can be traced back to Viking times. A custom that remains to this day is that the owners of the black-faced sheep that wander freely around the village hold common right, just as their predecessors did before them. Surprisingly the common land in the village was once used as a small golf course. Mallyan Spout waterfall (pictured on the previous page) can be reached from the footpath beside the Mallyan Hotel which leads down into West Beck gorge. The path can be a little tricky and is often wet but is well worth the effort. The parish church of St Mary's (left) is seen here on a crisp, clear winter's day.

Goathland lies on the 24-mile stretch of the North York Moors Railway which runs from Pickering to Grosmont. The picturesque station has its own signal box and it is one of very few stations on the line with two tracks. At the north end of the platform passengers can enjoy a superb view of the line as the train makes a steep climb from Beck Hole and Darnworth.

Rosedale

Rosedale is a long extended valley located in the heart of the North York Moors. It stretches out in a south-easterly direction from Westerdale Moor and Danby High Moor towards Hartoft End and Cropton Forest. The river Seven flows throughout its length gathering water from the numerous moorland springs and streams. The railbed of the disused Rosedale Mineral Railway is clearly visible around the perimeter of the dale and stunning views of the valley can be enjoyed from many of the moorland paths and in particular from Chimney Bank Top. The photograph (right), looking down the valley, was taken after heavy snow, from the road near the Lion Inn on Blakey Ridge.

Rosedale birdlife

The North of England, and in particular the North York Moors and Pennines, are very popular regions for game shooting. Vast areas of forest and moorland are sensitively managed and farmed so that game birds such as pheasant, partridge and grouse can co-exist in a sustainable environment. There is much debate about how the pheasant came to be introduced into Britain – possibly by the Normans in the 11th century or perhaps earlier by the Romans. Among game birds, only the grey partridge and the quail are native to Britain.

Rosedale Abbey

Although this delightful village is called Rosedale Abbey it has never had an abbey, but instead it was the site of a small Cistercian nunnery. Today, only a stone turret remains. The village owes its development to the fact that there were good deposits of ironstone around the head of the dale and 19th-century mine relics are still to be seen here. The village is very popular with visitors and has many attractions including a tea shop, a wild flower and herb nursery, a nine-hole golf course, and a national park information centre. The Rosedale Show (above) takes place every August and is an event that the whole community looks forward to each year.

Rosedale Walking

The village benefits from a national park information centre which is located at the Abbey Store and Tea Room (above). This makes an ideal starting point for exploring the village and the local moors. A short walk north of the village takes you to the slopes of North Dale from where there is a breathtaking panoramic view over Rosedale and the surrounding countryside.

The internationally renowned glassblower Stephen Gillies and artist Kate Jones run a very successful glassblowing business and gallery in the village. Much of their inspiration comes from the beauty of their rural location.

The Church of St Lawrence (left) is at the heart of the village.

Hole of Horcum

This unusual feature is a huge natural amphitheatre hollowed out of the heather-clad moor situated beside the A169 Pickering to Whitby road. Legend has it that "The Devils Punchbowl", as it is known locally, was made by a giant named Wade who scooped out the rocks and earth, tossing them two miles east to Blakey Topping. A very popular circular walk from the roadside car park goes down through the centre of the basin and on to take in the lovely villages of Lockton and Levisham, the latter of which has an excellent inn. The walk passes by this derelict farm cottage (left) which is situated at Low Horcum. It can be quite a strenuous hike, so it is reassuring to know that there is often a mobile tea van in the car park during the summer months.

Hackness

From earliest times, visitors have been captivated by the timeless charm of this quiet and beautiful village. Hackness was first mentioned in the *Ecclesiastical History of the English People* written by the Venerable Bede in the early eighth century. Bede described how Saint Hilda, abbess of Whitby and an active figure in the early English church, founded a nunnery in Hackness in 680AD, the year of her death.

St Peter's Church (below), houses a priceless Anglo-Saxon cross. When it was discovered in the

1830s it was being used as a gatepost! The cross is one of the finest examples of Anglo-Saxon Northumbrian sculpture.

The village is ideally suited for touring the area since it lies only five miles from the coast and the seaside resorts of Whitby and Sandsend. The Dalby Forest Drive is only a few minutes from the village by car, and close by Raincliffe Woods, Throxemby Mere and the River Derwent provide a wide variety of enticing walks for ramblers. The lovingly tended gardens of the stone cottages (above) in the centre of the village look magnificent in the late afternoon spring sunshine.

Lastingham

The village of Lastingham is a peaceful haven nestling comfortably amidst glorious scenery on the southern edge of the North York Moors and is the ideal place to stroll and relax. The area around Lastingham has much to offer with attractions such as Eden Camp Modern History Museum near Malton, the Flamingo Land theme park, Hutton Le Hole Folk Museum and many castles, stately homes, abbeys and churches.

The village is perhaps best known for the magnificent and historic Crypt Church of St Mary, with its unique and ancient crypt, which was built around 1078, as a shrine to St Chad and St Cedd who founded a Celtic monastery on this site around 645. The crypt is thought to be the only one in England to have an apse (rounded end) together with a chancel, nave and side aisles. The beautiful 14th-century stained-glass windows (right) are in the north aisle.

The farmer's dog (above) is often seen patrolling this area of the village, and can be relied upon to bark and make a fuss of walkers as they set off up the hill. Its bark is most definitely worse than its bite!

Levisham

The picturesque village of Levisham is located in the heart of the North York Moors National Park and is an attractive stop on the North York Moors Railway. The village nestles above the quiet and winding wooded valley of Newton Dale, seven miles north of Pickering. Its village green is unusually wide and is lined with characterful stone cottages and farm buildings.

Levisham attractions

The small church of St John the Baptist lies at the top of the village where the road and a footpath, which meanders across woods and fields, leads to the railway station in the bottom of the valley. Levisham station is set in the secluded and scenic Newton Dale Valley, which has a wide variety of wildlife and flowers along Pickering Beck. Birdwatchers often see hawks, woodpeckers, nuthatches, wagtails and kingfishers here. Newton Dale Hall is a walker's request stop on the steam train and a starting point for many lovely walks. The station has been used as the location for a range of television programmes including *All Creatures Great and Small, Poirot, Sherlock Holmes* and *Brideshead Revisited.*

Lockton

The rural hamlet of Lockton lies just north of the busy A169 Pickering to Whitby road, 4 miles (6km) north-east of Pickering. This unspoiled village has rural charm

in abundance and comes complete with free-range chickens and ducks, which are often to be seen waddling and scurrying around farm buildings on the main street.

Nearby there are excellent walks in Cropton Forest and along Levisham Beck, as well as the Dalby Forest drive. The Green Beacon Youth Hostel in the village is Britain's first eco-friendly youth hostel – it boasts a green roof and its showers are heated by solar panels. The hostel is full of environmental resources and is very popular with walkers. The Church of St Giles (left) has a 14th-century tower, and a medieval nave and chancel. There is also an ancient well in the village. Many of the locations used in *Heartbeat* can be found in this area.

Cropton

The little village of Cropton nestles on the southern edge of Cropton Forest, north of Wrelton on the A170 Helmsley to Pickering road. At the top of the village main street stands Cropton village well, a reminder of a bygone era. The well (right) was restored in 1988 when the remains of the winding gear were found nearby. A raised platform now covers the well and a sign states that it is over 300ft deep. The well was capped around 1920, possibly after piped water was introduced to the village. When the well was in use its water was reputed to be the best in the district and it would be brought to the surface in buckets on an endless rope system. To the east of the village

lies St Gregory's Church (left) which has a 10th-century cross in its graveyard. The following rhyme may link the village cross to the well:

> On Cropton cross there is a Cup
> And in that cup there is a sup
> Take that cup and drink that sup
> And set the cup on Cropton cross top

The New Inn at Cropton is 200 years old and is at the heart of village life. This family-run business is in the enviable position of owning its own brewery. Their Cropton Ales, including Scoresby Stout and the legendary Cropton 2-pints, have a very well-earned reputation.

Val Barnaby is a local artist. From her garden (above) she enjoys a spectacular view of the moors.

Cropton Forest

At just over 9,000 acres (3,600ha), Cropton Forest is mainly coniferous woodland set on the edge of the North York Moors, to the north of the village of Cropton. Its vast swathes of conifers produce about 20,000 tonnes of timber each year. Cropton is a very accessible forest, with a campsite, forest cabins and educational outdoor activity centres. The area provides a vital habitat for wildlife in the north of England and a very attractive environment for the many thousands of visitors who flock to the forest each year. Roe deer are very common in the area and red deer are occasionally seen in the north of the forest. The Forestry Commission began planting Scots pine and Japanese larch as early as 1929 and after the Second World War the Government initiated a massive planting scheme to help support the nation's depleted timber stocks. Cropton Forest was cast as the Forbidden Forest in the *Harry Potter* films.

Troutsdale

Situated 4 miles (6km) north of Snainton on the A170 Pickering to Scarborough road, Troutsdale and Rosekirk Dale Fens are designated Sites of Special Scientific Interest (SSSIs). These two areas of fenland are rich in spring and flush fen which grows well in the local area due to energy-rich springs which flow from the Corallian limestone underground. Fen systems like these are rare nationally and are only found in areas of Oxfordshire, Norfolk, Anglesey and North Yorkshire. Rushes, sedges, valerian, meadowsweet, meadowthistle and several species of orchid all flourish in this area. These fen beds and the rich green surrounding moorland makes Troutsdale a haven of peace and seclusion away from the hustle and bustle of local market towns. The gaggle of ducks (right) was photographed at Manor House Farm and (far right) cattle graze at Middle Farm, beyond which can be seen Troutsdale Brow Plantation.

Dalby Forest

The forest is situated on the southern slopes of the North York Moors
National Park and is accessed from Thornton Le Dale on the A170
Helmsley to Scarborough road. It mainly consists of pine and spruce
with many broadleaf trees such as beech, ash, oak, hazel and alder.
There are numerous clear springs in the forest running both north and
south and everywhere burial mounds and linear earthworks are a clue
to prehistoric life. The forest is crisscrossed by a network of minor
roads and cycle trails including the 9 mile (14.5km) Dalby Forest Drive
which can be accessed from the north via minor roads through

Hackness and
Langdale End. The
forest has a visitor
centre and car park
near the village of
Low Dalby. An
Astronomical Centre
and Observatory has
recently been added.
The forest is home to
birds such as Canada
geese, crossbills and
the elusive nightjar, a
summer visitor. Roe
deer are plentiful and
badgers, the symbol
of the forest, can
sometimes be spotted
as night descends.

Pickering

The busy and elegant market town of Pickering is located on the southern edge of the North York Moors where the A170 Thirsk to Scarborough road crosses the A169 Malton to Whitby road. It was originally a Celtic town dating from the 3rd century BC, and has a motte-and-bailey castle with Norman remnants. In the centre of the town is Beck Isle Museum of Rural Life, housed in a Grade 2 listed Regency mansion. The museum has 27 galleries and visitors are transported back through time as they pass through a wide variety of recreated settings including a cobblers' shop, blacksmiths, chemists' shop, dairy and village store. Of particular interest is the gallery which features the work of local photographer Sydney Smith who captured the atmosphere of rural life in and around Pickering in the late 19th and early 20th centuries. He is thought of as a successor to Frank Meadow Sutcliffe of Whitby. The Church of St Peter & St Paul (below) has some rare medieval paintings uncovered in the middle of the 19th century.

Pickering Steam

A major annual attraction is the Pickering Traction Engine Rally. Held on the showground, it is a four-day event with literally hundreds of lovingly restored and spectacular steam engines, vintage tractors, miniature steam engines, vintage and classic cars, fairground organs, military vehicles and motorcycles. The extravaganza of steam and fun appeals to people of every age, as can be seen in the photograph (below). Billed as the north's biggest steam event, the show has two vast arenas which stage several live shows. There are also army displays, Punch and Judy shows, a road run to Pickering and a fireworks display.

Thornton Le Dale

Thornton Le Dale lies just east of Pickering on the A170 Scarborough road.
In the centre of the town close to the crossroads is a small green, a market cross
and stocks. The village has gift shops, tea rooms, and a large tench pond near
the main car park; alongside the roads to Malton and Scarborough a
shimmering stream tumbles over a bed of cobbles. The thatched cottage (right)
is possibly one of the most photographed cottages in North Yorkshire.
Sammy Stenton of Easthill Farm is pictured (left) with her award-winning
Ryeland ewe at Thornton Le Dale Show where she won champion sheep "in
any other breed" class in 2004. In the same year Sammy won female champion
and reserve overall in the Ryeland class at the Great Yorkshire Show in Harrogate.

North York Moors West

THE NORTH YORK MOORS is a place where it is possible to unwind and enjoy some of the finest landscapes in Britain. Considerably drier than the Pennine moors to the west, the windswept purple heather-clad moors, lush green dales and vast expanses of woodland are characteristic of this unique area.

In the west the national park is bounded by the Hambleton and the Cleveland Hills. James Herriot, the author, once described the breathtaking view from Sutton Bank as the finest in England. Walk just a few miles along the escarpment from the national park visitor centre at the top of Sutton Bank and it is very easy to see just what he meant. Over eight centuries ago the abbot St Aelred, in describing the magnificent Rievaulx Abbey, just north of Helmsley, said "Everywhere peace, everywhere serenity, and a marvellous freedom from the tumult of the world." It is without doubt these very same experiences that compel visitors to return again and again to this captivating region.

Above: Bilsdale Silver Band and, *left*, Farndale

Kildale

The Kildale Agricultural and Horticultural Show was first established in 1881 and continues to be a major event for the farming community in the area each year. There is always something for the whole family at this hugely popular event, from show jumping, vintage vehicles, fancy dress, birds of prey or performances by silver bands. In 2004 the children's fancy dress competition was judged by William Hague, MP for Richmond, and his wife Ffion.

In April 1858 a railway station opened at Kildale on the North Yorkshire and Cleveland Railway. In the early 1900s the station won many awards for its floral displays. By the 1960s the station had become an unstaffed halt, the passing loop was lifted, and sadly almost all of the buildings were demolished leaving Kildale station with only fragments of its former rural charm.

Cricket

Kildale cricket club's ground (right) is in a glorious setting on the northern fringe of the North York Moors, on the road leading to the village of Commondale. The club plays in the Langbaurgh league.

Castleton

Situated in the upper Esk Valley, the linear village of Castleton sits proudly on a high ridge, where the lush green secluded valleys of Westerdale and Danby Dale come together on the northern fringe of the North York Moors. The settlement is steeped in history. The village hall, built in 1869, was called the Temperance Hall until 15 years ago – a throwback to the days when Temperance Societies, aiming to discourage alcohol, existed in nearly every settlement. The village has a

Quaker graveyard with gravestones dated from 1815 to 1944. A quick survey reveals that the majority of names on the stones have the surname of Puckrin. Remains of the old castle, built by Robert De Brus, are now part of a large house. Most of the castle was dismantled in

1216, and around 1240 some of the stones were used to restore Danby Church. The Castleton Show (left) draws huge crowds to see the show jumping and the road race. The distant view of the village in winter (above), was taken from Castleton Rigg looking north-east towards Danby Park Wood and Haw Rigg.

Westerdale

The monument named Young Ralph Cross (above) stands proud, next to the symbol marking the geological centre of the North York Moors; in 1974 it was adopted as the emblem of the national park. The cross was erected in the 18th century where an earlier named cross, Crux Radulph, once stood. Today the cross marks the point where the minor road into Westerdale joins the Hutton Le Hole to Castleton road at Rosedale Head. Records of the cross go as far back as 1200 and in 1550 it was constructed of wood. It is said that the present cross was erected in memory of a destitute traveller who died from exhaustion. A Danby farmer called Ralph discovered him and later decided to erect a cross where he found the body.

There is clear evidence on the moor above Dale View in Westerdale that the area has been inhabited since at least the Bronze Age. At Cairnfield around one hundred individual cairns and traces of metal workings have been discovered including an axe-hammer and other prehistoric remains.

Bilsdale

Fangdale Beck village (above) set in the heart of Bilsdale has a very unusual green telephone box and lies just west of the B1257 Helmsley to Stokesley road, between Bilsdale West Moor and Bilsdale East Moor. There are many excellent walks up and over the moors from this sleepy hamlet. Walk east to Bransdale or west to Snilesworth Moor and enjoy some of the finest scenery in northern Britain. Bilsdale has one of

the oldest buildings on the North Yorks Moors. The Old Sun Inn, also known as the Spout House, is a 16th-century cruck-framed cottage – a building with a curved timber supported roof. Built in 1550 it has been used as both a farmworker's cottage and shoemaker's workshop. It was opened as a licensed inn in 1774 and provided refreshment until it closed in 1914 when the Sun Inn was built across the yard. The Spout House is located 8 miles (12km) north of Helmsley on the B1257.

Bilsdale Silver Band (right) conducted by Dick Blackford, are seen here entertaining a packed audience at the Chop Gate Village Hall, at their annual Christmas Concert 2004. The evening included carol singing, poetry, stories, mince pies and solo performances from mezzo soprano Kirsten Mercer.

Blakey Ridge

The views from Blakey Ridge across both Rosedale to the east and Farndale to the west are quite simply breathtaking, particularly after heavy snow. This early morning photograph, taken from the side of the Helmsley to Castleton road, just north of the Lion Inn, reveals the head of Rosedale valley in all its splendour. The distant ridge, Nab Scar, just below Sturdy Bank, is where the dismantled railway bed runs around the east rim of Rosedale.

The Lion Inn is a tourist honeypot, where real ales, a cosy atmosphere and good food can always be guaranteed. Each year in July the music festival draws thousands of visitors to this stunning setting to enjoy the event where live bands and musicians perform on stage in the pub car park.

Blakey Ridge walking

The world famous coast-to-coast trail from St Bees in Cumbria to Robin Hood's Bay, devised by Alfred Wainwright, takes in Blakey Ridge. The 24-mile (38km) stretch from Clay Bank over Blakey Ridge, and then on to Grosmont, goes through remote and mostly uninhabited moorland. Another long-distance walk, the Lyke Wake Walk, a 41-mile (67km) route that passes by the Lion Inn, was founded in October 1955, making it one of the oldest established challenge walks in the country. It traverses the east to west watershed of this moorland area and follows Bronze Age burial mounds from near Osmotherly on the western edge of the moors to Ravenscar on the coast.

Bransdale

Bransdale is one of the North York Moors' best-kept secrets. Running north to south, between Farndale and Bilsdale, and approximately 7 miles (12km) north of Helmsley, it is a jewel of a dale, consisting of a few scattered farmsteads and cottages set in glorious scenery. At the head of the dale the tiny picturesque St Nicholas Church, and Bransdale Lodge, have a beautiful setting, lying just below Bransdale Moor on a south-facing wooded hillside. Walk or cycle around this delightful dale and you will discover names such as Toad Hole, Spout House, Groat Hill, Cow

Syke and Bransdale Mill. Bill Horner (left) has lived in the dale for over 40 years and loves the area passionately. He now spends a lot of his free time helping his son on a nearby farm. The red grouse, a wild game bird, feeds primarily on young heather and in the photograph (left) appears almost black against the snow.

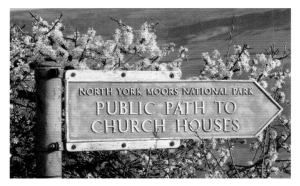

Farndale

The tiny and picturesque hamlet of Church Houses (above) nestles between the mighty Rudland Rigg and Blakey Ridge in glorious scenery at the heart of this much-loved dale. Perhaps best known for its wild daffodils in spring, Farndale attracts up to 40,000 visitors each April. The daffodil walk follows the valley bottom beside the river Dove, from Low Mill to Church Houses and the welcoming Feversham Arms. Pictured above, in spring, Church Houses and the distant winding minor road leading up to Blakey Ridge, were photographed from Daleside Road at the foot of Horn Ridge. A footpath (left) leads down from Daleside Road to Church Houses where walkers can savour fabulous views of the distant Potter's Nab and High Blakey Moor.

Gillamoor

The pretty village of Gillamoor lies 2.5 miles (4km) north of Kirby Moorside on the minor road that links Fadmoor to Hutton Le Hole. The village is famously known for its Surprise View at the eastern end of the hamlet, beside St Aidan's Church. The view of lower Farndale from this point is captivating and memorable whatever the season.

To the right, early morning winter mist slowly drifts northwards along the bottom of Douthwaite Dale and (below), in spring, the steep east-facing bank is festooned in a sea of wildflowers. The tiny church was rebuilt single-handedly by James Smith of Farndale in 1802; in the centre of the village can be found a very unusual four-faced sundial. There are many footpaths leading from the village both into the valley and up over the moors and a wide variety of birds can be seen in the area, including lapwings, curlews, snipe, fieldfares and finches.

Rievaulx Abbey

Traditionally Cistercian abbeys were built on an east-west axis, but because of the steep slope at Rievaulx a north-south alignment was adopted. Like all Cistercian houses the location was deliberately secluded from the outside world and this particular site in the depths of the narrow river Rye valley must have provided the monks and lay brethren with a haven of peace and solitude. The 13th-century church is reputed to have been one of the finest monastic churches in northern Britain and thankfully remains substantially intact. The abbey site is now owned and run by English Heritage, whereas Rievaulx Terrace and Temples (right), situated on an escarpment above the abbey, is owned by the National Trust. From this elevated position tremendous views of the abbey and valley are to be enjoyed. Recent archaeological discoveries show that the monks once ate wild strawberries and that there used to be a flourishing iron industry at the site.

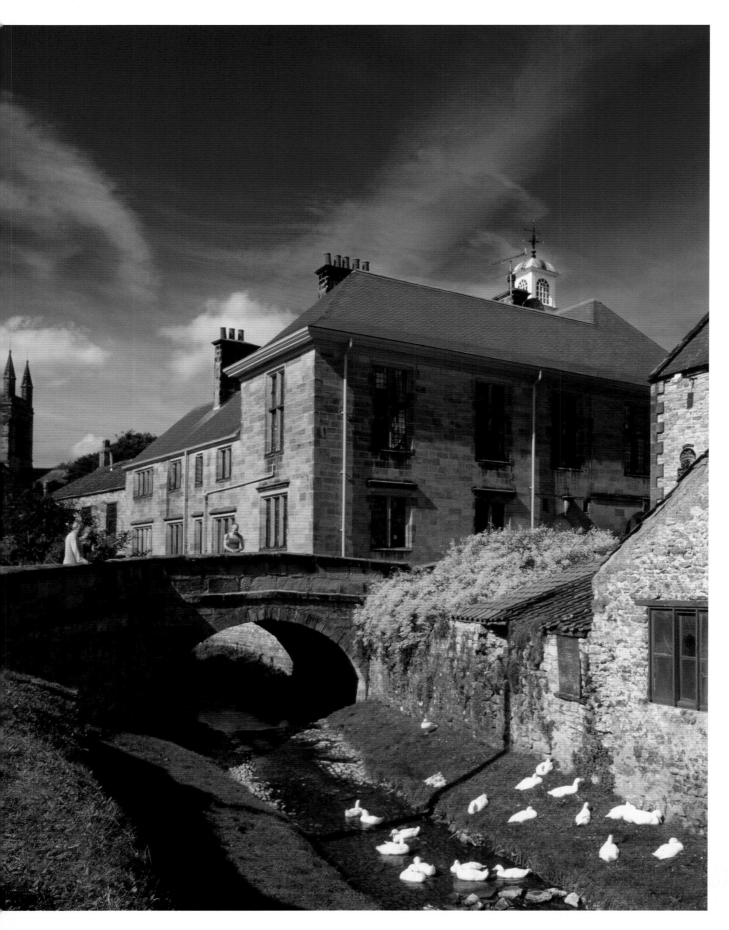

Helmsley

This is one of the prettiest country towns in North Yorkshire. Located on the Thirsk to Scarborough road, Helmsley is a very popular destination and an ideal centre for touring the local area. The market square is surrounded by a wide variety of gift shops, pubs, restaurants and galleries and on most weekends there is a lively atmosphere. A pretty stream runs through the town at the back of the market square (left) complete with stone arch bridge; a resident large flock of white ducks are often to be seen waddling up and down.

The poet William Wordsworth stayed at the Black Swan Inn in the centre of the town when courting Mary, his future wife. Helmsley Castle is a spectacular ruin and once guarded the Rye Valley. The early 13th-century castle is surrounded by a formidable double ditch cut from solid rock. It was once known as Furstan Castle. Sir Charles Duncombe purchased the castle after it was rendered useless by Oliver Cromwell and it has subsequently been owned by the Earls of Feversham who are descended from Sir Charles. The Feversham family live in the Vanbrugh-built mansion in nearby Duncombe Park on the edge of the village.

The Ryedale Show

The Ryedale and Pickering County Show is a very important annual event for the area, and the ideal opportunity for old friends to meet and catch up on local news. The show is held each year at Welburn Park near the market town of Kirkbymoorside just off the A170 Helmsley to Pickering road, close to the village of Welburn. When these photographs were taken, showgoers were enjoying a blisteringly hot day.

St Gregory's Minster in Kirkdale, a very early medieval church a short walk north of the showground, is well worth visiting. Hidden away in a wooded valley beside Hodge Beck the church has a secluded setting and is of historic and architectural interest. Kirkdale's most famous monument is an Anglo-Saxon sundial set into the outer wall of the nave.

Kirkbymoorside

The market town of Kirkbymoorside is considered by many to be the gateway to the North York Moors. A sizeable town situated on the busy A170 Helmsley to Pickering road, market day is Wednesday when traders from the area come together to sell their goods. It has a wide variety of shops and services and yet enjoys a tranquil atmosphere helped by the fine ornate Yorkshire stone buildings that line the main street. Locals call the town "Kirby" and are fortunate to live in a town with such an appealing aspect, surrounded by green rolling hills. The population is well served on the sporting front as the town's amenities include an 18-hole golf course as well as a cricket ground and squash courts. All Saints Church (above) is set back from the main street, and photographed here from a recently landscaped area on the edge of town. Manor Vale Woodland (left) is an ancient woodland that was bought by the council in 1993; it is now actively managed for wildlife and recreation.

Hawnby

The remote village of Hawnby, set in the Hambleton Hills in Upper Ryedale just north-west of Rievaulx, is something of an enigma. It is a village of two halves, which are split by a steep hill.

The village is a stopping-off point on the Cleveland Way long-distance footpath. Just west of the village, the footpath links Helmsley in the west with Filey in the east – a distance of just over 100 miles. On the nearby Hambleton Hills there are traces of the old Hambleton Drove Road, a high-level route along which cattlemen would drive their animals to the market towns further south.

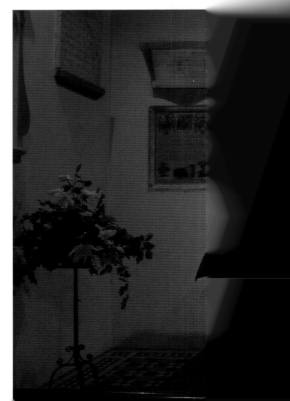

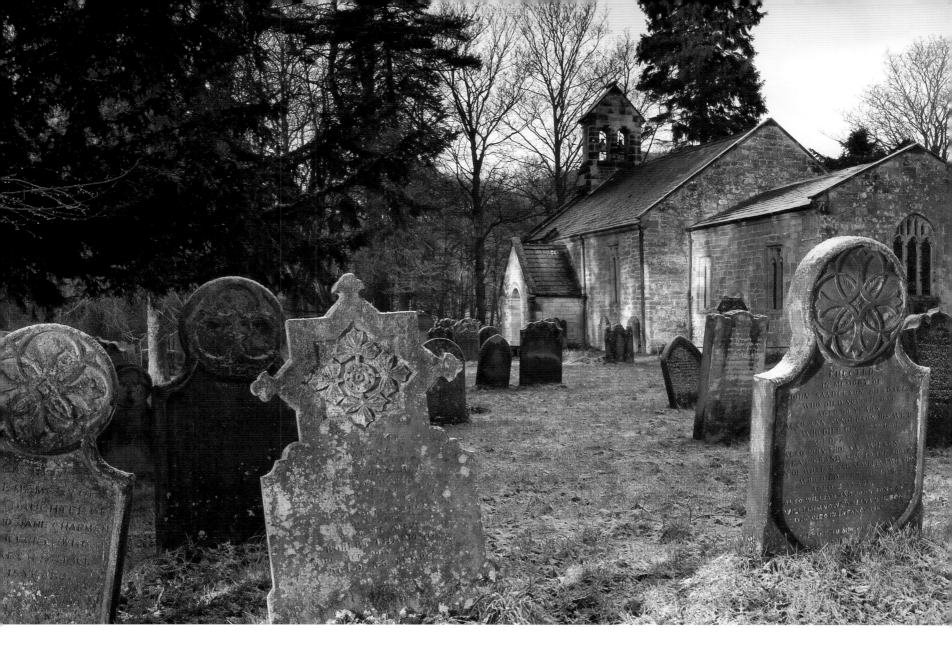

Hawnby Church

The church of All Saints is isolated and some distance from the village. Historical sources record that in the middle of the 18th century two men, Chapman and Cornforth, experienced vivid dreams of God speaking to them. They subsequently met the preacher John Wesley and were inspired to become the first Methodists in the neighbourhood. Unfortunately their homes at the top of the hill were owned by Lord Tancred who was an Anglican and very much opposed to their cause. After being expelled from the village they decided to resettle down in the valley by the bridge, and so the village developed in two halves!

Old Byland

The tiny and peaceful hamlet of Old Byland is located just west of Rievaulx Abbey in the south-west corner of the North Yorks Moors. The village consists of a few stone cottages and farm buildings surrounding a small village green. The church of All Saints is steeped in history and there has been a church of one kind or another on this site since Saxon times. Following the Norman Conquest the area was ravaged by William the Conqueror's army. The Domesday Book records for 1086 state that only two settlements, Helmsley and Old Byland, survived and that there was "a priest and a wooden church" in the village. Today the church is very well cared for, as can be seen by the splendidly restored weather vane.

Boltby

Nestling in a deep narrow valley just west of the
Hambleton Hills and two miles north of Gormire
Lake, Boltby is a delightfully quiet and peaceful
village. Its name derives from the Danish *boltebi* and
it is mentioned in the Domesday Book. The village
street is lined with attractive stone and brick
cottages; in its centre is Holy Trinity Church.

The village has a population of approximately
170, and an "on demand" bus service on Mondays to
the bustling market town of Thirsk. Walkers along
the Cleveland Way footpath should consider
taking a slight detour in order to explore this
lovely hamlet in its tranquil setting. A pretty stone
bridge straddles Gurtof Beck which runs under
the road, and occasionally over it, after heavy rain!

Sutton Bank

Views from Sutton Bank over the Vale of York and Mowbray towards the Yorkshire Dales are deservedly considered to be some of the finest in the north of England. The Hambleton Escarpment rises abruptly to a height of around 1,000ft (300m) and you can often see for more than 30 miles (50km). Roulston Scar and Hood Hill (left) are bathed in warm evening light as the sun sets over the dales far away to the west and (above) Gormire Lake is silhouetted by a dramatic sky stirred up by strong winds sweeping impatiently across the Vale of York. Gormire, which is semi-circular in shape, is one of only a few true lakes in Yorkshire and Gormire Rigg is a glacial feature creating a retaining bowl-shaped bank behind the lake. Unusually, there are no streams in or out of the lake. Just beyond Roulston Scar lies the well-known landmark the White Horse of Kilburn, built by local teacher John Hodgson and his pupils in 1857.

The Cleveland Way

Whitestone Cliff on the Cleveland Way footpath looking north towards the village of Boltby. The Cleveland Way starts in the market town of Helmsley and traverses the upland ridge on the edge of the North York Moors before reaching the coast at Saltburn by Sea. It then continues along the Heritage Coast and ends at Filey – a distance of 110 miles (177km). The footpath is really two walks in one, the first a walk along high moorland while the second is a walk along one of the most outstanding sections of coastline in Britain.